Easy Bake Oven Recipes

101 Cheap and Easy Recipes for Young Bakers

Pat Herbert

Table of Contents

FROSTINGS and GLAZINGS 79

SNACKS and DESSERTS 109

Introduction

Forward

A child's oven (such as the Easy-Bake Oven) is a young girl's dream gift and a wonderful hobby. It's fun to bake like mom and even produce fairly good results. It's also practical while learning to:

1. Recognize and measure ingredients
2. Read instructions
3. Become familiar with kitchen utensils
4. Work safely around the kitchen and oven.

There's also the added benefit of spending quality time with your child as she (or he) learns the basics of baking.

Unfortunately, the recipe packages or cake mixes you can purchase for baking in these ovens can be very expensive; about $7 for two cakes or $3.50 for a single layer cake. This book will relieve you of that expense and allow you and your child to experiment, making the hobby much more enjoyable.

Included in this introduction is your first recipe, which is how to make your own mixes from a boxed cake mix and how to make a "basic" cake. The typical yield will be 20-25 single layer cakes from a boxed cake mix. These sell for anywhere from $0.50 at your dollar store to $3.00 at a specialty store, which works out to about as low as 2-3 cents a cake, or perhaps as high as 12-15 cents a cake, which is still much less expensive than $3.50.

Included also are 101 other "scratch" recipes; listed above. We've tried them all with good success rates. The index is linked to each recipe page so you just need to tap the recipe name and it will jump to that spot in the book. The recipes are listed alphabetically and sorted into nine groups, including:

- ➤ 6 Bar recipes
- ➤ 7 Bread and Biscuit recipes
- ➤ 5 Brownie recipes
- ➤ 24 Cake recipes
- ➤ 22 Cookie recipes
- ➤ 15 Frosting and Glazing recipes
- ➤ 8 Main Dish recipes
- ➤ 6 Pie recipes
- ➤ 8 Snack and Dessert recipes

Safety precautions and oven directions should be included with your oven. However, there are some precautions and recommendations included in this book so you will have the very best experience possible with these recipes.

Recommendations

1. Not absolutely required but why not make the recipes as healthy as possible by using quality butter or coconut oil for both the recipes and for "greasing" the pans, instead of using margarine or shortening in the recipes or cooking spray for greasing the pans. That said however, margarine, shortening or a spray will work just as well.

2. I recommend using organic ingredients whenever possible. There is no reason why a fun hobby can't be as healthy for your child as you can make it.

3. A recipe may call for a "prepared" pan. This refers to a buttered and floured pan.

4. The average temperature of a child's oven is about 350F, so if you want to test a recipe first, you can bake it in your regular oven at 350F for the time specified.

5. Always preheat your oven for about 20 minutes, or as you gather the ingredients for the recipe. The oven should be preheated BEFORE mixing wet and dry ingredients to avoid some of the mixes from "rising" too much before baking.

6. The outside of the oven may become very hot, so keep a safe distance please.

7. Use heat resistant gloves or other material when working around the oven or inserting and removing oven pans. A spatula or tongs also work very well.

8. If you're making brownies, remember that brownies do not look the same as a cake during baking. Brownies should not take longer than about 17 minutes to bake. Check them with a

toothpick to ensure the desired result. Insert a toothpick in the center after baking for about 14 minutes. If it comes out clean, the brownie is done. If there are traces of uncooked batter on the toothpick, let it continue baking for another minute. Check with a clean toothpick every minute until the toothpick comes out with no trace of uncooked batter.

9. I sincerely hope you enjoy this book and are able to spend many quality hours following these recipes and perhaps even experiment with a few ideas of your own.

10. If you notice any errors in the book and would like to tell me about it, just leave a little note in the review and I will fix it. Your Kindle should be updated automatically once the fix is complete.

11. If you have the time and inclination, please leave an honest review for the author. Reviews are the mainstay of authors and we depend on your reviews to become successful authors. Thank you in advance.

How to make inexpensive cake mixes:

Ingredients and notes with recommendations:
- 1 package boxed cake mix from directions below
    - Notes:
        - o Although any cake mix will probably work, we prefer Duncan Hines cake mixes as they seem to work the best.
        - o Start with Classic White, French Vanilla and Dark Chocolate Fudge which should pretty well guarantee success right at the start.
        - o Under the "Cakes" section in this book, you will find a make-ahead recipe for White, Vanilla (or Yellow) and Chocolate cakes, using the following directions.

Directions and recommendations:
1. Sift the cake mix into a large bowl.
2. Precisely measure 1/4 cup of cake mix into sealable containers or re-sealable baggies.
    - Notes:
        a. We use Ziplock snack bags.
        b. Or, you could just use 1/4 cup out of the box as you need it.
3. Label for future reference.
    - Notes:
        a. We use a magic marker right on the plastic bag or a piece of painter's tape.
        b. If you just use 1/4 cup out of the box, then the box should be labeled because it will now not make a full "regular" cake.
4. Store for future use.
    - Note:
        a. We store the snack bags in a shoe box with labeled cardboard dividers to separate the different mixes.

Directions to prepare each mix and recommendations:

1. Preheat your oven for 20 minutes.

    Notes:

    a. Do not pre-mix the cake batter while waiting for the oven to preheat. It may rise too high and stick to the top of the oven.

    b. The outside of the oven may become very hot, so hands clear, please.

2. Lightly coat the oven pan with butter.
3. When the oven has heated, pour the 1/4 cup of dry mix into a bowl.
4. Add 2 tablespoons of water.

    Note:

    a. Not all cake mixes and flours are the same, so you may need more or less water to make a well-blended mixture. Use your own judgment and adjust the recipes in this book accordingly. Because all ovens are different, recipes are normally guidance, not precision.

5. Mix thoroughly.
6. Spread the cake mix evenly in the pan.
7. Bake for 16-18 minutes.

    Notes:

    a. Baking times may differ depending on your oven model, age and instructions. Don't be afraid to experiment a bit.

    b. Cakes are usually done when they are lightly browned or they start to pull away from the pan sides.

8. Remove from oven and cool for 5 minutes.

    Note:

    a. The pan will be very hot. Remove carefully with gloves, spatula or tongs.

9. Spread frosting of your choice on the cake if desired.
10. Decorate with sprinkles or other cake decorations if desired.

BARS

6-Layer Bar

Ingredients:
- 2 tablespoons butter
- 1/3 cup graham wafer crumbs
- 2 tablespoons semisweet chocolate chips
- 2 tablespoons butterscotch chips
- 2 tablespoons flaked coconut
- 2 tablespoons chopped walnuts
- 2 tablespoons sweetened condensed milk

Directions:
1. Melt butter in an oven baking pan.
2. Remove from oven.
3. Sprinkle graham cracker crumbs evenly over butter.
4. Layer chocolate and butterscotch chips.
5. Add a layer of flaked coconut.
6. Sprinkle walnuts on top.
7. Pour condensed milk evenly over everything.
8. Bake about 15 minutes.

Apple Bar

Ingredients:
- 3 tablespoons flour
- 1 tablespoon crushed cornflakes (or other similar cereal)
- 1 tablespoon soft butter
- 1 teaspoon sugar
- 2 teaspoons apple jelly
- 1/8 teaspoon cinnamon; optional

Directions:
1. In a bowl, mix flour, cinnamon, cereal, butter and sugar until crumbly.
2. Reserve 2 tablespoons of the crumbly mixture.
3. Press remaining mixture firmly into pan.
4. Spread with jelly.
5. Sprinkle reserved crumbly mixture over jelly.
6. Press gently with fingers.
7. Bake for 18 minutes.
8. Cool.
9. Cut into slices.

Chocolate Peanut Butter Bars

Ingredients:
- Peanut butter
- Graham crackers
- Mini chocolate chips

Directions:
1. Spread a thin layer of peanut butter on a graham cracker.
2. Top with mini chocolate chips.
3. Bake for 5 minutes to melt the chocolate chips.
4. Remove and spread the softened chocolate chips.
5. Allow bar to cool slightly before eating.

Granola Bars

Ingredients:
- 1/4 cup rolled oats
- 3 teaspoons all-purpose flour
- 1/8 teaspoon baking soda
- 1/8 teaspoon vanilla extract
- 2 teaspoons softened butter
- 1 teaspoon honey
- 1 teaspoon packed brown sugar
- 1 teaspoon semisweet mini chocolate chips
- 1 teaspoon raisins

Directions:
1. Combine oats, flour, soda, vanilla, butter, honey and sugar.
2. Add in chocolate chips and raisins.
3. Lightly press the mixture into a greased and floured oven pan.
4. Bake for 10 minutes.
5. Let cool for 10 minutes.
6. Cut into bars.

Oatmeal Fruit Bars

Ingredients:
- 1 tablespoon soft butter
- 6 teaspoons brown sugar
- Dash salt
- 1/4 cup flour
- 1/8 teaspoon baking soda
- 2 tablespoons quick cooking rolled oats
- 3 tablespoons milk
- 2 teaspoons apple sauce or marmalade

Directions:
1. Mix butter, sugar and salt until creamed.
2. Add flour, baking soda, oats, and milk.
3. Mix well until it forms soft dough.
4. Place 1/2 of the mixture in a greased pan.
5. Press down in pan with fingertips or back of spoon.
6. Spread with 2 teaspoons apple sauce or marmalade
7. Bake about 20 minutes.
8. Let cool and cut into bars.

Recipe makes 2 pans

Raspberry Bars

Note:

To make Strawberry Bars, substitute the raspberry jam for strawberry jam.

Ingredients:
- 3 tablespoons flour
- 1 tablespoon crushed cornflakes
- 1 tablespoon soft butter
- 1 teaspoon sugar
- 2 teaspoons raspberry jam

Directions:
1. Mix together flour, cornflakes, butter and sugar in a bowl until crumbly.
2. Reserve 2 tablespoons of mixture.
3. Press remaining mixture firmly into oven pan.
4. Spread with jam.
5. Sprinkle reserved mixture over jam.
6. Press down gently.
7. Bake for 18 minutes.
8. Remove from oven to cool.
9. Cut into bars.

BREADS and BISCUITS

Basic Biscuits

Ingredients:
- 1/4 cup biscuit mix (such as Bisquick)
- 4 teaspoons milk

Directions:
1. Combine biscuit mix and milk with a fork until smooth.
2. Drop by 1/2 teaspoonful onto lightly greased baking pan.
3. Bake until the biscuits are golden brown.

Blueberry Danish

Ingredients:
- 1/4 cup biscuit mix (such as Bisquick)
- 1/2 tablespoon butter
- 3/4 teaspoon sugar
- 4 teaspoons milk
- 1/2 tablespoon blueberry pie filling

Directions:
1. Combine the biscuit mix, butter and sugar.
2. Mix until crumbly.
3. Add the milk and stir well, until a soft dough forms.
4. Drop by 1/2 teaspoonful onto lightly greased baking pan.
5. Indent each drop by pressing your thumb into the middle.
6. Fill each indent with blueberry pie filling.
7. Bake until the biscuits are golden brown.
8. Frost with vanilla frosting.

Cheesy Glazed Biscuits

Ingredients:
- 1/2 cup biscuit mix (such as Bisquick)
- 2 tablespoons plus 2 teaspoons milk
- 2 tablespoons shredded cheddar cheese
- 1 tablespoon parmesan cheese

Directions:
1. Stir together biscuit mix, milk and cheeses until a soft dough forms.
2. Drop by 1 teaspoonful onto an ungreased pan.
3. Bake in oven for 15 minutes or until bottoms are lightly browned.
4. Remove the pan from oven.
5. Top with garlic glaze.

Cherry Danish Biscuits

Ingredients:
- 1/4 cup biscuit mix (such as Bisquick)
- 1/2 tablespoon butter
- 3/4 teaspoon sugar
- 4 teaspoons milk
- 1/2 tablespoon cherry pie filling

Directions:
1. Combine biscuit mix, butter and sugar.
2. Mix until crumbly.
3. Stir in milk until dough forms then beat another 15 strokes.
4. Drop by 1/2 teaspoonful onto lightly greased baking pan.
5. Indent by pressing thumb into middle.
6. Fill indent with cherry pie filling.
7. Bake in oven until golden brown.
8. Drizzle vanilla frosting over the top of each biscuit.

Cinnamon Bread Pudding

Ingredients:
- 4 slices white bread
- 1 egg
- 1/2 cup milk
- 1/4 teaspoon vanilla
- 4 tablespoons sugar

For the topping:
- Cinnamon
- 2 teaspoon milk
- 1/2 teaspoon butter

Directions:
1. Break bread into small pieces.
2. Mix egg, milk, vanilla, sugar and bread pieces together in a bowl.
3. Grease 3 pans lightly with butter.
4. Fill pans 1/2 full and press down.
5. Sprinkle lightly with cinnamon.
6. Add 1/3 of the milk and 1/3 of the butter on top of each pudding.
7. Bake 20 to 25 minutes.

Makes 3 Puddings

Scones

Ingredients:
- 1 tablespoon sour cream
- 1/8 teaspoon baking soda
- 1/3 cup all-purpose flour
- 1 tablespoon sugar
- 1/8 teaspoon baking powder
- 1/8 teaspoon cream of tartar
- 1/8 teaspoon salt
- 1 tablespoon butter
- 1 tablespoon raisins; optional

Directions:
1. Grease and flour an oven pan.
2. Blend the sour cream and baking soda in a bowl and set it aside.
3. Mix the flour, sugar, baking powder, cream of tartar and salt together.
4. Cut in the butter.
5. Stir in the sour cream mixture until just moistened.
6. Mix in the raisins.
7. Knead the dough briefly on a lightly floured surface.
8. Roll or pat the dough until it's about 1/2" thick and round.
9. Cut the round into wedges and place them on a buttered baking sheet.
10. Bake in the oven for 15 minutes.
11. Let cool.

Strawberry Biscuits

Ingredients:
- 1/4 cup biscuit mix (such as Bisquick)
- 1/2 tablespoon butter
- 3/4 teaspoon sugar
- 4 teaspoons milk
- 1/2 tablespoon strawberry pie filling

Directions:
1. Combine biscuit mix, butter and sugar.
2. Mix until crumbly.
3. Add milk and stir the mixture until a soft dough forms.
4. Drop by 1/2 teaspoonful onto a lightly buttered baking pan.
5. Indent each biscuit by pressing your thumb into its middle.
6. Fill each indent with strawberry pie filling.
7. Bake until golden brown.
8. Drizzle vanilla frosting over the top of each biscuit.

BROWNIES

Notes:
1. Remember that brownies do not look the same as a cake during baking.
2. Brownie baking time may vary, depending on the model of your oven.
3. Older ovens cook at approximate 375F and will take about 12 minutes.
4. Newer ovens tend to cook at around 350F so they'll take approximately 14-16 minutes.
5. Do not cook longer than 17 minutes.

Brownies Mix #1

Ingredients:
- 2-1/2 tablespoons flour
- 2 teaspoons sugar
- 1 teaspoon coconut oil (or olive oil)
- Pinch baking soda
- Dash salt
- 1 teaspoon baking cocoa
- 1/8 teaspoon vanilla extract
- 4 teaspoons milk
- 2 teaspoons chocolate syrup

Directions:
1. In a small bowl combine all of the ingredients.
2. Mix well until smooth.
3. Pour batter into greased and floured cake pan.
4. Bake 12-15 minutes or according to your oven directions.
5. Remove from oven and cool before cutting.

Brownie Mix #2

Ingredients:
- 2 tablespoons sugar
- 2-1/2 tablespoons flour
- 1 teaspoon oil
- 1/8 teaspoon baking powder
- 1/8 teaspoon vanilla extract
- 2 teaspoons chocolate syrup
- 2 teaspoons milk
- 1 teaspoon baking cocoa

Directions:
1. Blend all ingredients until the batter is smooth.
2. Pour batter into greased and floured cake pan.
3. Bake 14-17 minutes or until done.

Graham Brownie Mix

Ingredients:
- 2-1/2 tablespoons flour
- 2 teaspoons sugar
- 1 teaspoon coconut oil
- Pinch baking soda
- Dash salt
- 1 teaspoon baking cocoa
- 1/8 teaspoon vanilla extract
- 4 teaspoons milk
- 2 teaspoons chocolate syrup
- 1/3 cup graham wafer crumbs
- 1 teaspoon cocoa
- 2 tablespoons chopped nuts
- 1 tablespoon sweetened condensed milk

Directions:
1. Blend all ingredients thoroughly.
2. Spread in well-buttered pan.
3. Bake 12-15 minutes or until done.

Mint Chocolate Brownies

Ingredients:
- 2 tablespoons white sugar
- 1 tablespoon softened butter
- 3 tablespoons chocolate syrup
- 2 tablespoons all-purpose flour

Directions:
1. Grease a baking dish.
2. Cream together sugar and butter until smooth.
3. Stir in chocolate syrup.
4. Stir in flour until blended.
5. Spread batter evenly into prepared pan.
6. Bake in oven for about 15 minutes.
7. Cool completely in pan.
8. Top with Peppermint Frosting

Double Fudge Brownies

Ingredients:
- 2 1/2 tablespoons sugar
- 1 teaspoon oil
- 1/8 teaspoon vanilla extract
- 4 teaspoons chocolate syrup
- 1/4 teaspoon baking coco
- 2 1/2 tablespoons flour

Directions:
1. Stir all ingredients together until the batter is smooth.
2. Pour the batter into a greased and floured pan.
3. Bake for 15 minutes.
4. Cool 5 minutes.
5. Cut & serve.

CAKES

Banana Cream Cake

Ingredients:
- 6 tablespoons flour
- 4 teaspoons sugar
- 1/4 teaspoon baking powder
- Dash salt
- 6 teaspoons milk
- 2 teaspoons butter
- Frosting of choice
- 3 tablespoons banana cream pudding mix

Directions:
1. Mix flour, sugar, baking powder and salt.
2. Add milk and butter.
3. Stir until batter is smooth
4. Add banana cream pudding mix.
5. Pour the batter into a buttered and floured oven pan.
6. Bake for 12 to 15 minutes or until sides of cake separates from pan.
7. Remove and cool.

Makes 2 Layers

Banana Split Cake

Ingredients:
- 1 yellow cake mix
- 5 tablespoons fruit cocktail syrup
- 1 small banana
- 3 teaspoons vanilla ice cream
- 1 tablespoon each of pineapple syrup, strawberry syrup, and chocolate syrup
- Whipped cream
- 1 cherry
- Pecan or walnut pieces

Directions:
1. Stir cake mix and fruit cocktail syrup together until well blended and smooth.
2. Pour batter into a round, buttered cake pan.
3. Bake for 18 - 20 minutes or until cake is done.
4. Slice cooled cake in half to make two, even, round cake layers.
5. Place banana halves on bottom layer of cake, & trim overhanging pieces.
6. Place 3, 1-tablespoon scoops of ice cream across the banana halves.
7. Top each scoop with a different topping (pineapple, strawberry, chocolate syrup).
8. Add the top layer of cake.
9. Garnish the top of the cake with whipped cream, cherry and nut pieces.
10. Decorate your cake plate with ice cream toppings.

Berry Cake

Ingredients:
- 4 yellow cakes (see Yellow Cake page)
- 1/4 cup heavy, liquid whipping cream
- 1/3 cup blueberries
- 2 strawberries
- Cake Mate decorating gel tubes; optional

Directions:
1. Bake 4 yellow cake layers per directions and let cool.
2. Whip heavy whipping cream with 2 teaspoons of sugar until it holds soft peaks.
3. Place one cake layer on cake plate.
4. Spread 1/4 of prepared whipped cream on the layer.
5. Top with 8 blueberries around edge of cake and 1 blueberry in center.
6. Place second cake layer on top of first.
7. Spread 1/4 of prepared whipped cream on cake.
8. Top with 8 blueberries around edge of cake and 1 blueberry in center.
9. Place third cake layer on top of second.
10. Spread 1/4 of prepared whipped cream on third layer.
11. Top with 8 blueberries around edge of cake and 1 strawberry in center.
12. Place remaining cake on top of third.
13. Spread remaining whipped cream on fourth cake layer.
14. Top with 8 blueberries around edge of cake
15. Top with 1 strawberry in the center.
16. Create designs on top of cake and around berries using decorating gel.

Makes one 4-Layer Cake

Birthday Cake

Ingredients:
- 4 teaspoons flour
- 2 teaspoons cocoa powder
- 1 tablespoon sugar
- 1/8 teaspoon baking powder
- 1 dash salt
- 1/8 teaspoon vanilla
- 4 teaspoons water
- 2 teaspoons vegetable oil
- Frosting of your choice

Directions:
1. Combine all ingredients except frosting in a small bowl.
2. Stir until the batter is smooth and chocolate colored.
3. Pour the batter into a buttered and floured cake pan.
4. Bake for 13 to 15 minutes or until the cake pulls away from the sides of the pan.
5. Remove cake from oven and cool.
6. Cover with a frosting of your choice.

Makes 1 Layer

Blueberry Shortcake

Ingredients:
- 1/4 cup biscuit mix
- 5 teaspoons milk
- Blueberries
- 1 tablespoon sugar
- 1/8 teaspoon cinnamon
- Whipped cream

Directions:
1. In a bowl, combine the biscuit mix and milk, using a fork.
2. Divide into two portions.
3. Roll one at a time on a floured surface to fit a pan.
4. Place each roll in a buttered pan.
5. Bake about 10 minutes.
6. Let cool and transfer to a clean bowl.
7. In a separate bowl, combine the blueberries, sugar and cinnamon.
8. Pour the blueberry mixture over the cake.
9. Top with the whipped cream.

Butterscotch Trifle Cake

Ingredients:
- 6 tablespoons boxed yellow cake mix (such as Duncan Hines)
- 2 tablespoons milk
- 4 tablespoons butterscotch pudding
- 3 tablespoons whipped cream

Directions:
1. Mix the yellow cake mix with 2 tablespoons of milk until smooth.
2. Bake in 2 prepared round cake pans for 15 minutes each.
3. Let cool.
4. Cut into small squares.
5. Fold pudding and whipped cream together.
6. In trifle dish or glass bowl arrange pieces from one cake in bottom.
7. Cover with pudding mixture.
8. Repeat.
9. Chill until served.

Makes 2 servings

Carrot Cake

Ingredients:
- 2 yellow cake mixes
- 1/8 teaspoon ground cinnamon
- 2 pinches ground nutmeg
- 2 pinches ground ginger
- 1 tablespoon shredded carrots
- 2 teaspoons drained, crushed pineapple
- 1 teaspoon of a beaten egg
- 2 1/2 teaspoons water
- Cream cheese frosting

Directions:
1. Butter and flour 2 pans.
2. Combine all ingredients except frosting until completely mixed.
3. Pour 1/2 of mix into each pan.
4. Bake cakes for 9 – 11 minutes each.
5. Remove from pan and allow to cool.
6. Apply cream cheese frosting between layers, top and around cake.

Chocolate Cake

Ingredients:
- 1/4 cup of boxed chocolate cake mix
- 2 tablespoons water

Directions:
1. Lightly coat an oven pan with butter.
2. Combine the cake mix and water.
3. Mix thoroughly.
4. Spread evenly in the pan.
5. Bake for 16 - 18 minutes.
6. Remove from oven and cool for 5 minutes.
7. Spread frosting of your choice on the cake.
8. Decorate with sprinkles or other cake decorations.

Chocolate Cake

(from scratch)

Ingredients:
- 6 teaspoons flour
- 4 teaspoons sugar
- 1/4 teaspoon baking powder
- 1 teaspoon unsweetened cocoa
- 1 pinch salt
- 3/4 teaspoon butter
- 6 teaspoons milk

Directions:
1. Mix all dry ingredients
2. Slowly add milk and butter, mixing until smooth.
3. Pour into a greased baking pan.
4. Bake 15 minutes.

Makes 1 serving

Crazy Cake

Ingredients:
- 4 1/2 teaspoon flour
- 3 teaspoon sugar
- 1/4 teaspoon cocoa
- 1 dash salt
- 1/8 teaspoon baking soda
- 1 1/2 teaspoon butter
- 1/8 teaspoon vanilla
- 1/8 teaspoon vinegar
- 1 tablespoon water

Directions:
1. Mix the 5 dry ingredients together.
2. Add the 4 wet ingredients one at a time, stirring gently until mixed thoroughly.
3. Bake in oven about 10 minutes.

Cherry Cheesecake

Ingredients:
- 1 sugar cookie dough, prepared
- 2 tablespoons cherry pie filling

Cream Cheese Filling
- 2 tablespoons cream cheese
- 2 teaspoons confectioners' sugar

Directions:
1. Press cookie dough evenly into prepared pan.
2. Bake for 15 - 20 minutes, until golden brown.
3. Cool in pan on wire rack.
4. In large mixing bowl, mix cream cheese with confectioners' sugar.
5. Spread cream cheese filling on cooled cookie dough.
6. Cover with cherry pie filling.

Cinnamon Coffee Cake

Ingredients:
- 1/3 cup biscuit mix (such as Bisquick)
- 2 3/4 teaspoons white sugar
- 1 teaspoon butter
- 1/2 teaspoon of a slightly beaten egg
- 1/4 teaspoon cinnamon
- 1 tablespoon milk

Directions:
1. Stir all ingredients together until just moistened.
2. Pour into greased and floured oven pan.
3. Bake for 15 minutes. Let cool.

Elegant Tea Cakes

Ingredients:
- 1/4 cup all-purpose flour
- 1/4 teaspoon baking powder
- 1/8 teaspoon salt
- 2 teaspoons sugar
- 2 teaspoons butter
- 4 teaspoons milk
- 1 teaspoon multi-colored cookie decorations

Directions:
1. Mix together flour, baking powder, salt, sugar and butter until dough looks like medium-sized crumbs.
2. Slowly mix in the milk to create dough.
3. Form the dough into a loose ball and divide it into 4 pieces.
4. Place the dough pieces on a greased sheet or pan.
5. Sprinkle the decorations over the dough.
6. Push the decorations into the dough with your fingers.
7. Bake 20 minutes.

Makes 4 tea cakes

Orange Nut Cake

Ingredients:
- 1/2 cup white cake mix (such as Duncan Hines)
- 1 teaspoon orange zest
- 4 tablespoons water
- 1/2 tablespoon chopped pecans
- 1/2 tablespoon coconut
- Orange glaze

Directions:
1. Mix 1/4 cup white cake mix with 1/2 teaspoon of orange zest and 2 tablespoons water.
2. Bake for 12 minutes in prepared round cake pan.
3. While the first cake layer is baking, prepare an orange glaze and set aside.
4. Remove first pan from oven and invert onto a small plate.
5. Mix the remaining white cake mix with remaining orange zest and water.
6. Bake for 12 minutes in another prepared round cake pan.
7. Pierce first layer with fork several times to help absorb the glaze.
8. Drizzle 1 1/2 teaspoons of the orange glaze over the top of the first layer.
9. Place second layer on first layer and drizzle remaining orange glaze over all.
10. Sprinkle the finished cake with nuts and coconut.

Peanut Butter Cake

Ingredients:
- 1 yellow cake mix (or 1/4 cup boxed vanilla cake mix)
- 1 tablespoon peanut butter
- 2 tablespoons milk

Directions:
1. Prepare two oven pans.
2. Combine all ingredients, stirring until batter is smooth.
3. Pour into prepared pans.
4. Bake for 12 to 15 minutes or until sides separate from pan.
5. Remove and cool.
6. Cover with frosting of your choice.

Make 2 cakes, or 1 double layer cake

Pink Velvet Cake

Ingredients:
- 5 tablespoons flour
- 1/4 teaspoon baking powder
- 1/8 teaspoon salt
- 5 teaspoons red sugar crystals
- 1/4 teaspoon vanilla
- 4 teaspoons butter
- 8 teaspoons milk

Directions:
1. Stir together all ingredients until batter is smooth and pink.
2. Pour 3 tablespoons of batter into greased and floured cake pan.
3. Bake 15 minutes.
4. Repeat for second layer.
5. Optional; frost with frosting of your choice.

Suggested Frostings:
Sparkling frosting
Strawberry frosting
White frosting with a drop of red food coloring

Makes 2 Layers

Shortcake

Ingredients:
- 1/4 cup biscuit mix (Bisquick)
- 5 teaspoons milk

Directions:
1. Combine biscuit mix and milk using a fork.
2. Divide into two portions.
3. Roll one portion at a time on a floured surface to fit pan.
4. Place each portion in a greased pan.
5. Bake about 10 minutes.
6. Allow to cool.

Snowman Cake

Ingredients:
- Enough pre-made white cakes mixes for 3 layers (or 3/4 cup boxed cake mix)
- 1/2 cup white frosting mix
- Mini marshmallows
- Red licorice
- Chocolate kisses
- Mini chocolate chips
- Gummy worms
- Coconut flakes

Directions:
1. Bake and cool 3 layers of round cake.
2. Arrange layers side-by-side on a plate to make a snowman shape.
3. Layer with white frosting.
4. Arrange marshmallows to cover the surface of each layer.
5. Use mini chocolate chips for eyes, nose and mouth.
6. Cut red licorice for a scarf
7. Use gummy worms for arms.
8. Sprinkle coconut flakes for "snow".

Strawberry Cake

Ingredients:
- 1 package yellow cake mix or 1/2 cup boxed cake mix
- 2 teaspoons strawberry Jell-O powder
- 2 tablespoons milk

Directions:
1. Butter and flour two oven pans.
2. Combine all ingredients, stirring until batter is smooth.
3. Pour into prepared pans.
4. Bake for 12 to 15 minutes or until sides separate from pan.
5. Remove and cool.
6. Frost with strawberry frosting.

Strawberry Cheesecake

Ingredients:
- 1 batch sugar cookie dough, prepared as directed (see sugar cookies)

For Cream Cheese filling
- 2 tablespoons cream cheese
- 2 teaspoons confectioners' sugar
- 2 tablespoons strawberry pie filling

Directions:
1. Press cookie dough evenly into oven pan.
2. Bake for 15 - 20 minutes, until golden brown.
3. Cool in pan on wire rack.
4. Mix together cream cheese, confectioners' sugar and pie filling.
5. Spread cream cheese filling on cooled cheesecake.
6. Cover with strawberry pie filling.

Strawberry Shortcake

Ingredients:
- 1/4 cup biscuit mix (Biscuick)
- 5 teaspoons milk
- Strawberries
- Whipped cream

Directions:
1. Combine biscuit mix and milk using a fork.
2. Divide into two portions.
3. Roll one at a time on a floured surface to fit pan.
4. Place each in a prepared pan.
5. Bake about 10 minutes or until golden brown.
6. Let cool.
7. Place in a bowl, top with strawberries and whipped cream

Vanilla (Yellow) Cake

Ingredients:
- 1/4 cup of boxed vanilla (or French vanilla) cake mix
- 2 tablespoons water

Directions:
1. Preheat your oven for 20 minutes.
2. Lightly coat the oven pan with butter.
3. When the oven has heated, pour the 1/4 cup of mix into a bowl.
4. Add 2 tablespoons of water.
5. Mix thoroughly.
6. Spread the cake mix evenly in the pan.
7. Bake for 16-18 minutes.
8. Remove from oven and cool for 5 minutes.
9. Spread frosting of your choice on the cake.
10. Decorate with sprinkles or other cake decorations.

Vanilla (Yellow) Cake Mix
(from scratch)

Ingredients:
- 6 teaspoons flour
- 4 teaspoons sugar
- 1/4 teaspoon baking powder
- 1 pinch salt
- 3/4 teaspoon butter
- 6 teaspoons milk
- 2 drops of vanilla

Directions:
5. Mix all dry ingredients
6. Slowly add milk and butter, mixing until smooth.
7. Pour into a greased baking pan.
8. Bake 15 minutes.

Makes 1 serving

White Cake

Ingredients:
- 1/4 cup of boxed white cake mix
- 2 tablespoons water

Directions:
1. Preheat your oven for 20 minutes.
2. Lightly coat the oven pan with butter.
3. When the oven has heated, pour the 1/4 cup of mix into a bowl.
4. Add 2 tablespoons of water.
5. Mix thoroughly.
6. Spread the cake mix evenly in the pan.
7. Bake for 16-18 minutes.
8. Remove from oven and cool for 5 minutes.
9. Spread frosting of your choice on the cake.
10. Decorate with sprinkles or other cake decorations.

COOKIES

Angel Cookies

Ingredients:
- 6 teaspoons butter
- 3 teaspoons sugar
- 3 teaspoons brown sugar
- 1 pinch salt
- 1/4 cup flour
- 1/8 teaspoon cream of tartar
- 1/8 teaspoon baking soda

Directions:
1. Cream together butter, sugars and salt.
2. Mix in flour, cream of tartar, and baking soda until smooth.
3. Drop by teaspoonful onto a baking sheet.
4. Bake 5 - 7 minutes.

Makes one dozen one-inch cookies

Apple Cookies

Ingredients:
- 1/4 cup softened unsalted butter
- 1/2 cup granulated sugar
- 1/2 tablespoon grated apple
- 1 cup all-purpose flour
- 1/8 teaspoon salt
- 1/8 teaspoon baking soda
- 3 tablespoons granulated sugar
- Red food coloring

For Icing:
- 1/2 cup confectioners' sugar
- 2 tablespoons apple juice

Directions:
1. In a large bowl, cream the butter and 1/2 cup sugar together.
2. Add the grated apple and mix well.
3. In another bowl, sift together the flour, salt and baking soda.
4. Add to the sugar/butter mix.
5. Turn the dough onto a floured cutting board.
6. Knead until smooth and
7. Divide in half.
8. Wrap separately in waxed paper and chill until firm, about 1 hour.
9. Mix the 3 tablespoons sugar with the food coloring.
10. Shape each chilled log half into an 8-inch long log.
11. Roll logs in colored sugar to coat.
12. Wrap and chill until hard, about 3 hours or overnight.
13. Butter and flour the baking pans.
14. Unwrap and slice the logs into 1/4 inch thick rounds.
15. Place two rounds in each prepared pan.
16. Bake until the cookies start to brown around the edges, about 20 minutes.
17. Cool the pans on a wire rack.
18. When cookies are cool, transfer them to wire racks.

For Icing:
1. Mix confectioners' sugar and apple juice.
2. Brush cookies with icing and let cool.

Candied Cherries Cookies

Ingredients:
- 1/2 cup softened butter
- 1/2 cup packed brown sugar
- 1/2 teaspoon vanilla
- 1 1/2 cups all-purpose flour
- 1 1/2 teaspoons baking powder
- 1/4 teaspoon salt
- 3 tablespoons finely chopped candied cherries
- 3 tablespoons chopped nuts

Directions:
1. In bowl, cream butter with sugar and mix in vanilla.
2. In a small bowl, combine flour, baking powder and salt.
3. Stir the mixture into the butter/sugar mixture.
4. Stir in cherries and nuts.
5. Divide in half.
6. Wrap separately in waxed paper and chill until firm, about 1 hour.
7. Remove 2 halves from fridge and shape into two 8-inch logs.
8. Wrap again and chill until hard, about 3 hours or overnight.
9. Unwrap and slice the two logs into 1/4" rounds.
10. Place two rounds in prepared pans.
11. Bake 18 - 20 minutes.
12. Cool pans on wire rack.

Caramel Chocolate Cookies

Ingredients:
- 2 tablespoons softened butter
- 2 tablespoons white sugar
- 2 tablespoons packed brown sugar
- 1/4 teaspoon vanilla extract
- 1/4 cup all-purpose flour
- 1/8 teaspoon baking soda
- 1 tablespoon unsweetened cocoa powder
- 1/4 teaspoon white sugar for dipping
- 12 butterscotch mini chips

Directions:
1. Cream butter and sugars until fluffy and mix in vanilla.
2. Gradually add flour, baking soda and cocoa to the butter mixture, beating well.
3. Cover and chill at least two hours or overnight.
4. Divide dough into 4 parts and refrigerate.
5. Work with one part at a time, leaving in the fridge until needed.
6. Divide each part into six pieces.
7. Press each piece of dough around two butterscotch mini chips.
8. Roll into balls and dip tops into the dipping sugar.
9. Place sugar side up on buttered baking sheets.
10. Bake for 8 minutes.
11. Let cool 5 minutes then remove to wire racks to cool completely.

Chocolate Chip Cookies

Ingredients:
- 1 tablespoon sugar
- 1 tablespoon packed brown sugar
- 2 teaspoons butter
- 1/8 teaspoon baking powder
- 1/8 teaspoon vanilla extract
- 1 teaspoon water
- 3 tablespoons all-purpose flour
- 4 teaspoons semi-sweet chocolate chips

Directions:
1. Stir together the sugars and butter.
2. Add the baking powder, vanilla, water and flour, stirring until well mixed.
3. Mix in the chocolate chips.
4. Roll the dough between your fingers and make twelve, 1/2 inch balls.
5. Place a few balls on a buttered and floured sheet.
6. Bake 10 to 12 minutes.

Cranberry Cookies

Ingredients:
- 1/4 cup softened butter
- 1/2 cup packed light brown sugar
- 1/2 teaspoon vanilla extract
- 1/4 teaspoon baking soda
- 1/4 teaspoon cream of tartar
- 1/4 teaspoon salt
- 1 1/4 cups flour
- 1/4 cup finely chopped blanched almonds
- 1/4 cup coarsely chopped cranberries
- 1 teaspoon grated lemon rind

Directions:
1. Cream the butter and brown sugar until fluffy.
2. Beat in vanilla, baking soda, cream of tartar and salt.
3. Blend in flour & stir in remaining ingredients.
4. Divide in half, wrap separately and chill until firm, about 1 hour.
5. Shape each half into an 8-inch long log.
6. Roll logs in confectioners' sugar to coat.
7. Wrap each log in waxed paper and chill about 3 hours or overnight.
8. Unwrap, slice logs into 1/4-inch thick rounds.
9. Place two rounds in prepared pans.
10. Bake 18 - 20 minutes.
11. Cool pans on wire rack.

Cream Cheese Sugar Cookies

Ingredients:
- 2 tablespoons softened butter
- 2 tablespoons softened cream cheese
- 1/8 teaspoon salt
- 1/8 teaspoon almond extract
- 1/8 teaspoon vanilla extract
- 1/4 cup + 2 tablespoons all-purpose flour

Directions:
1. Combine all ingredients except flour and beat until smooth.
2. Add flour until well blended.
3. Chill overnight.
4. On a lightly floured surface, roll the dough to about 1/8-inch thickness.
5. Cut into desired shapes with lightly floured cookie cutters.
6. Refrigerate any remaining dough until ready to use.
7. Bake your cookie shapes for 7 to 10 minutes.
8. Cool cookies completely.
9. Top with frosting of your choice.

Gingersnap Cookies

Ingredients:
- 3 tablespoons butter
- 1/4 cup white sugar
- 1 tablespoon molasses
- 1/2 cup all-purpose flour
- 3/4 teaspoon ground ginger
- 1/4 teaspoon ground cinnamon
- 1/2 teaspoon baking soda
- 1/8 teaspoon salt
- 2 tablespoons white sugar for decoration

Directions:
1. Cream the butter and 1/4 cup white sugar until smooth.
2. Gradually beat in the molasses until well blended.
3. In a separate bowl, combine flour, ginger, cinnamon, baking soda and salt
4. Slowly stir the dry mix into the molasses mixture to form dough.
5. Roll the dough into 1-inch balls.
6. Roll these balls in the remaining sugar.
7. Place the coated cookies on an ungreased cookie sheets.
8. Bake 8-10 minutes.
9. Allow cookies to cool on cookie sheet for 5 minutes.
10. Place cookies on a wire rack to cool completely.

Oatmeal Cookies

Ingredients:
- 1/4 cup packed brown sugar
- 1/4 cup flour
- 1/4 teaspoon baking soda
- 1/2 cup quick oats
- 1/4 cup softened butter

Directions:
1. Blend all ingredients well.
2. Let sit 5 minutes.
3. Form dough into 1/2-inch balls.
4. Place on un-greased baking pan.
5. Press down lightly on each ball to flatten slightly.
6. Bake 7-10 minutes or until lightly browned.

Makes about 2 dozen cookies

Peanut Butter Cookies

Ingredients:
- 2 tablespoons butter
- 1/4 cup cocoa
- 1/2 cup sugar
- 1/4 cup milk
- Dash salt
- 1 teaspoon vanilla extract
- 1 tablespoon peanut butter
- 1 1/2 cups quick oats

Directions:
1. Melt the butter in a warming cup.
2. Stir in the cocoa until dissolved.
3. Stir in the sugar, milk and salt.
4. Add the vanilla, peanut butter and oatmeal and thoroughly combine.
5. Form into 12 cookies.
6. Bake for about 10 minutes or until lightly browned.

Makes 12 Cookies

Pecan Cookies

Ingredients:
- 8 tablespoons unsalted, softened butter (1 stick)
- 1/4 cup sugar
- 1/2 teaspoon vanilla extract
- 1 cup all-purpose flour
- Pinch of ground cinnamon
- Pinch of salt
- 1/2 cup coarsely chopped, toasted pecans
- Powdered sugar for dusting

Directions:
1. Cream the butter, sugar and vanilla together.
2. Add flour, cinnamon, salt and pecans to form stiff dough.
3. Turn dough onto a floured surface and form into an 8-inch log.
4. Wrap in waxed paper and refrigerate 3 hours or overnight.
5. Unwrap and slice dough into 3/8-inch rounds.
6. Place 2 rounds on each pan.
7. Bake until the cookies start to brown at the edges (about 20 minutes).
8. Cool pans on a wire rack.
9. When cooled completely, dust cookies with powdered sugar.

Potato Drop Cookies

Ingredients:
- 2 tablespoons butter
- 2 tablespoons sugar
- 2 tablespoons brown sugar
- 1/4 of a beaten egg
- 1/8 teaspoon vanilla extract
- 1/4 cup all-purpose flour
- 1/8 teaspoon baking soda
- 1/8 teaspoon salt
- 1/4 cup crushed potato chips

Directions:
1. Cream butter and sugars until fluffy.
2. Add remaining ingredients one at a time, mixing well.
3. Drop by the teaspoonful onto an ungreased pan.
4. Bake 8 - 10 minutes.
5. Allow cookies to cool on a baking sheet for 5 minutes.
6. Remove to wire rack to cool completely.

Raisin Cookies

Ingredients:
- 3 teaspoons sugar
- 1 1/2 teaspoons butter
- 1/8 teaspoon vanilla
- 3 teaspoons milk
- 6 teaspoons flour
- 1/8 teaspoon baking powder
- 1 tablespoon raisins

Directions:
1. Stir sugar and butter together until creamy.
2. Add in vanilla and milk, mixing well.
3. Add in flour and baking powder.
4. Add raisins.
5. Drop by 1/2 teaspoon of dough onto greased pan allowing room to spread.
6. Bake 5 - 7 minutes per batch.
7. Cool before serving.

Santa Cookies

Ingredients:
- 1/2 cup butter
- 1/2 cup sugar
- 1 tablespoon milk
- 1/2 teaspoon vanilla
- 1 1/4 cups all-purpose flour
- 1/2 cup finely chopped red candied cherries
- 1/4 cup finely chopped pecans
- 1/2 cup coconut flakes

Directions:
1. Cream butter and sugar until fluffy.
2. Add milk and vanilla, blending well.
3. Add flour, cherries and pecans to form stiff dough.
4. Turn onto floured surface and form into an 8" log.
5. Wrap in wax paper and refrigerate 3 hours or overnight.
6. Butter and flour baking pans.
7. Unwrap and slice the dough log into 1/4-inch rounds.
8. Place 2 rounds in each prepared pan.
9. Bake until the cookies start to brown around the edges (about 20 minutes).
10. Cool pans on wire rack.

Secret Chocolate Chip Cookie

Ingredients:
- 1 tablespoon white sugar
- 1 tablespoon firmly packed brown sugar
- 2 teaspoons butter
- 1/8 teaspoon baking powder
- 1/8 teaspoon vanilla extract
- 1 teaspoon water
- 3 tablespoon all-purpose flour
- 4 teaspoons semi-sweet chocolate chips

Directions:
1. Stir together the sugars and butter.
2. Add the baking powder, vanilla, water and flour, stirring until dough forms.
3. Mix in the chocolate chips.
4. Roll the dough between your fingers to make twelve 1/2-inch balls.
5. Place a few balls on a greased and floured sheet or pan with space between them.
6. Bake 10 to 12 minutes.
7. Repeat until all the cookies are baked.

Makes 12 cookies

Snowball Cookies

Ingredients:
- 6 teaspoons soft butter
- 3 teaspoons confectioners' sugar
- 1/8 teaspoon vanilla
- 1/4 cup flour
- Dash of salt
- 2 tablespoons finely chopped walnuts
- Confectioners' sugar for rolling

Directions:
1. Cream butter and confectioners' sugar until smooth.
2. Add vanilla, mixing well.
3. Mix in the flour and salt.
4. Add in walnuts and mix well.
5. Carefully shape into 1-inch balls.
6. Roll balls in confectioners' sugar.
7. Place 3 balls in each easy bake pan and flatten slightly with a fork.

Makes 10 - 12 cookies

Sugar Cookies

Ingredients:
- 7 teaspoons butter
- 7 teaspoons sugar
- Pinch of salt
- 1/8 teaspoon vanilla
- 1/4 cup flour
- 1/8 teaspoon baking powder

For Icing:
- 3 tablespoons powdered sugar
- Dash of salt
- 1 teaspoon hot water
- 1/2 teaspoon butter
- Sprinkles; optional

Directions:
1. Cream together butter, sugar, salt and vanilla.
2. Add flour and baking powder.
3. Mix until a ball of dough forms.
4. Roll out on a floured surface.
5. Use mini cookie cutters to cut out shapes.
6. Place cookies in buttered oven pan.
7. Bake for 5 minutes.
8. Allow cookies to cool before removing from oven.
9. Mix all the icing ingredients except the sprinkles.
10. Decorate the cookies with sprinkles while slightly warm.

Snow Mounds Cookies

Ingredients:
- 6 teaspoons soft butter
- 3 teaspoons confectioners' sugar
- 1/8 teaspoons vanilla extract
- 1/4 cup flour
- Dash of salt
- 2 tablespoons finely chopped walnuts
- 2-3 teaspoons confectioners' sugar for rolling

Directions:
1. Cream together the butter and 3 teaspoons confectioners' sugar.
2. Blend in vanilla, flour and salt.
3. Add walnuts and mix well.
4. Shape into 1-inch balls.
5. Place 3 balls onto a well-buttered pan.
6. Flatten slightly.
7. Bake 5 minutes.
8. When cool, roll in confectioners' sugar.

Makes 10 to 12 cookies

Sugar and Spice Cookies

Ingredients:
- 1 1/2 cups all-purpose flour
- 1/2 teaspoon baking powder
- 1/4 teaspoon ground nutmeg
- 1/4 teaspoon ground cinnamon
- 1/2 cup softened butter
- 1/4 cup sugar
- 1/4 cup packed brown sugar
- 1/4 teaspoon vanilla extract
- 1/4 teaspoon lemon extract
- 1/2 cup chopped nuts of your choice

Directions:
1. In a small bowl, combine flour, baking powder, nutmeg, and cinnamon.
2. Set this flour mixture aside.
3. In a medium bowl, cream the butter and sugars together.
4. Add vanilla and lemon extract, beating well.
5. Add the flour mix gradually, blending well.
6. Stir in the nuts.
7. Divide in half.
8. Wrap separately in waxed paper and chill about 1 hour or until firm.
9. Shape each half into an 8-inch log.
10. Wrap and chill about 3 hours or overnight.
11. Butter and flour the baking pans.
12. Unwrap and slice the dough logs into 1/4-inch rounds.
13. Place 2 rounds in each prepared pan.
14. Bake about 20 minutes or until the cookies start to brown at edges.
15. Cool pans on wire rack.

Makes 72 Cookies

Thumbprint Cookie

Ingredients:
- 1 tablespoon powdered sugar
- 2 tablespoons butter
- 1/4 teaspoon vanilla
- 1/2 teaspoon water
- 1/4 cup all-purpose flour
- Your favorite jelly or jam

Directions:
1. Stir together powdered sugar, butter, vanilla, water and flour until dough forms.
2. Roll the dough between your fingers to make twelve 1/2-inch balls.
3. Place a few balls at a time on an ungreased sheet or pan with space between them.
4. Press your thumb into the middle of each ball to make a thumb print.
5. Bake 10 to 12 minutes.
6. Repeat until all the cookies are baked.
7. When the cookies are cool, fill each thumb print with jam or jelly.

Makes 12 cookies

White Chocolate Cookies

Ingredients:
- 2 tablespoons softened butter
- 2 tablespoons packed brown sugar
- 2 tablespoons white sugar
- 1 teaspoon vanilla extract
- 1/4 cup all-purpose flour
- 1/8 teaspoon baking soda
- 3 tablespoons white chocolate chips
- 1/4 cup dried cranberries

Directions:
1. Cream the butter and sugars together until smooth.
2. Beat in vanilla extract.
3. In a separate bowl, combine flour and baking soda.
4. Fold into sugar mixture.
5. Mix in white chocolate chips and cranberries.
6. Drop by the teaspoonful onto buttered pans.
7. Bake for 8 - 10 minutes.
8. Remove while still doughy.
9. Cool 5 minutes.
10. Serve warm.

Vanilla Cookies

Ingredients:
- 1/4 cup butter
- 1/2 cup sugar
- 1/2 teaspoon vanilla
- 3/4 cup sifted flour
- 1/8 teaspoon salt
- 1/8 teaspoon baking powder
- 1/4 cup chopped nuts
- Powdered sugar

Directions:
1. Cream together butter, sugar and vanilla.
2. In a separate bowl measure flour, salt and baking powder, stirring well to combine.
3. Add gradually to butter mixture.
4. Add nuts and mix well.
5. Divide in half, wrap separately with waxed paper and chill until firm (about 1 hour).
6. Shape each half into an 8-inch log.
7. Wrap each log in waxed paper and chill until hard (about 3 hours or overnight).
8. Unwrap and slice logs into 1/4-inch rounds.
9. Place two rounds into prepared pans.
10. Bake until the cookies start to brown around the edges (about 20 minutes).
11. Cool pans on wire rack.
12. When cooled completely, dust with powdered sugar.

FROSTINGS and GLAZINGS

Buttercream Frosting
Make-Ahead Mix
(Divide ingredients by 8 to make an individual frosting)

Ingredients:
- 2 cups confectioners' sugar
- 3 tablespoons instant non-fat milk powder
- 6 tablespoons butter

Directions:
1. Combine confectioners' sugar and powdered milk, mix well.
2. Cut in butter with pastry blender.
3. Spoon about 1/3 cup mixture into each of 8 small containers or re-sealable bags.
4. Seal tightly and label with date and contents.
5. Store in refrigerator.
6. Use within 12 weeks.

Makes about 8 packages frosting

To use frosting:
1. Add 3/4 teaspoon water to 1 package butter cream frosting mix.
2. In a small bowl, combine the mix and water.
3. Stir well with a spoon until smooth and creamy.

Chocolate Frosting

(Divide ingredients by 8 to make an individual frosting)

Ingredients:
- 2 cups confectioners' sugar
- 3 tablespoons instant nonfat milk powder
- 1/2 cup unsweetened cocoa powder
- 6 tablespoons butter

Directions:
1. Combine all ingredients until mixture resembles crumbs.
2. Spoon about 1/3 cup of mixture into each of 8 small containers or re-sealable bags.
3. Seal tightly and label with date and contents.
4. Store in refrigerator.
5. Use within 12 weeks.

Makes 8 packages of Frosting

To use frosting:
1. Add 3/4 tsp. water to 1 pkg. chocolate frosting mix in a small bowl.
2. Combine well and stir with a spoon until smooth.

Makes about 1/4 cup

Cream Cheese Frosting
Make-Ahead Mix
(Divide ingredients by 8 to make an individual frosting)

Ingredients:
- 2 cup confectioners' sugar
- 4 1/2 teaspoons instant nonfat milk powder
- 3 tablespoons cream cheese

Directions:
1. Combine sugar and powdered milk, blending with a wire whisk.
2. Cut in cream cheese.
3. Spoon 1/3 cup mixture into each of 8 containers or re-sealable bags.
4. Seal tightly and label with date and contents.
5. Store in refrigerator for up to 2 weeks.

To use frosting:
1. Add 3/4 teaspoon water to 1 package cream cheese frosting mix.
2. Add a drop of almond extract.
3. Combine well with spoon until smooth and creamy.

Makes 1/4 cup of frosting - enough to frost a double layer cake
Great for carrot cake, pumpkin cake or spice cakes

Crystal Sugar Frosting

Ingredients:
- 4 teaspoons vegetable shortening
- 2/3 cup powdered sugar
- 1/4 teaspoon vanilla
- 1 teaspoon milk
- Colored sugar crystals; optional

Directions:
1. Mix together all ingredients until smooth and creamy.
2. Sprinkle with colored sugar crystals, if desired.

Garlic Glaze

Ingredients:
- 1 tablespoon butter
- 1/8 teaspoon garlic powder
- 1/4 teaspoon dried parsley

Directions:
1. Melt the butter in a warming tray.
2. Stir the garlic powder and parsley flakes into the melted butter.
3. Brush the mixture over warm biscuits (such as cheese biscuits).

Lemon Frosting

Ingredients:
- 1/4 cup powdered sugar
- 1 teaspoon lemon juice
- 1 teaspoon water

Directions:
1. Mix sugar, lemon juice and water together.
2. Stir until smooth.
3. Add water to thin if required.
4. Add more powdered sugar to thicken if necessary.

Makes frosting for 1 - 2 single layer cakes

Orange Glaze

Ingredients:
1. 1 tablespoon fresh squeezed orange juice
2. 1 tablespoon sugar
3. 1/2 teaspoon orange zest

Directions:
1. Mix all the ingredients together.

Peanut Butter Frosting

Make-Ahead Mix
(Divide ingredients by 8 to make an individual frosting)

Ingredients:
- 2 cups confectioners' sugar
- 3 tablespoons instant non-fat milk powder
- 6 tablespoons peanut butter

Directions:
1. Combine confectioners' sugar and powdered milk, mix well.
2. Cut in peanut butter with pastry blender.
3. Spoon about 1/3 cup mixture into each 8 small containers or re-sealable bags.
4. Seal tightly and label with date and contents.
5. Store in refrigerator.
6. Use within 12 weeks.

Makes 8 Packages

To use frosting:
1. Add 3/4 teaspoon water to 1 package Butter Cream Frosting mix in a small bowl.
2. Add a drop or two of vanilla if desired.
3. Stir well with a spoon until smooth and creamy.

Makes about 1/4 cup of frosting

Peppermint Frosting

Ingredients:
- 1/4 cup confectioners' sugar
- 1/2 cup butter
- 1/2 teaspoon peppermint extract

Directions:
1. Mix sugar, butter and extract until smooth.
2. Spread evenly over cooled brownies or cookies.
3. Chill until set.

Sparkling Frosting

Ingredients:
- 4 teaspoons butter
- 2/3 cup confectioners' sugar
- 1/4 teaspoon vanilla
- 2 teaspoons milk
- Colored sugar crystals for decoration

Directions:
1. In a small bowl, mix together butter, confectioners' sugar, vanilla and milk until smooth and creamy.
2. Spread 2 teaspoons of frosting on top of 1st layer of cake.
3. Add 2nd layer and continue frosting.
4. Sprinkle with colored crystal sugars.

Frosts a 2 layer cake

Strawberry Frosting

Ingredients:
- 1/4 cup confectioners' sugar
- 1 teaspoon strawberry drink powder
- 2 teaspoons water

Directions:
1. Combine confectioners' sugar and drink powder.
2. Add 2 teaspoons water and stir until smooth.
3. If frosting is too thick, add a little water.
4. If frosting is too thin, add a little powdered sugar.

Makes enough to frost two layers of cake

Vanilla Frosting #1

Ingredients:
- 1/4 c. confectioners' sugar
- 2 drops vanilla
- 1 teaspoon water

Directions:
1. Combine all 3 ingredients.
2. Mix until it reaches a smooth, desired consistency.

Vanilla Frosting #2

Ingredients:
- 4 teaspoons butter
- 2/3 cup powdered sugar
- 1/4 teaspoon vanilla
- 2 teaspoons milk

Directions:
1. In a small bowl, mix all ingredients together until smooth and creamy.
2. Spread 2 teaspoons of frosting on top of 1st layer of cake.
3. Add 2nd layer and continue frosting.

Watermelon Frosting

Make-Ahead Mix

(Divide ingredients by 8 to make an individual frosting)

Ingredients:
- 2 cups confectioners' sugar
- 3 tablespoon instant non-fat milk powder
- 1 teaspoon watermelon drink powder
- 6 tablespoons butter

Directions:
1. In a medium size bowl, combine sugar, milk powder and drink powder, stirring well.
2. Cut butter into mix.
3. Measure about 1/3 cup in each of 8 containers or re-sealable bags.
4. Store in refrigerator up to three months.

Makes 8 packages of watermelon frosting

To use frosting:
1. Add 3/4 teaspoon water to one package mix in a small bowl.
2. Mix until smooth.

White Frosting

Ingredients:
- 2 cups sifted confectioners' sugar
- 3 tablespoons instant nonfat milk powder
- 6 tablespoons butter

Directions:
1. Combine all ingredients, blending well.
2. Spoon about 1/3 cup of mixture into each of 8 small containers or re-sealable bags.
3. Seal bags tightly and label with date and contents.
4. Store in refrigerator.
5. Use within 12 weeks.

Makes 8 packages white frosting mix.

To use frosting:
1. Mix 3/4 teaspoon water with 1 package frosting in a small bowl.
2. Add a drop or two of vanilla if desired.
3. Stir well with a spoon until smooth and creamy.

Makes about 1/4 cup frosting

MAIN DISHES

Cheesy Potato Hot Dogs

Store bought hot dogs are already cooked. Your oven will warm them nicely.

Ingredients:
- 2 hot dogs
- 1/2 cup cooked mashed potatoes
- 1/4 cup grated cheddar or parmesan cheese

Directions:
1. Slice hot dogs into thirds.
2. Split hot dogs the long way but not quite all the way through.
3. Fill split opening with mashed potatoes.
4. Sprinkle top with cheese.
5. Bake about 15 minutes or until heated through and slightly browned on top.

Chicken Pizza

Your oven will not cook meat. Use only **cooked** chicken in this recipe.

Ingredients:
- 2 tablespoons all-purpose flour
- 1/8 teaspoon baking powder
- Dash of salt
- 1 teaspoon butter
- 2 1/4 teaspoon milk
- 2 tablespoons chopped **cooked** chicken
- 1 tablespoon barbeque sauce
- 1 1/2 tablespoons shredded mozzarella cheese

Directions:
1. Stir together flour, baking powder, salt and butter until dough looks crumbly.
2. Slowly add milk while stirring until dough forms.
3. Shape dough into a ball and place into a greased pan.
4. Use fingers to pat dough evenly over bottom of pan, then up sides.
5. Pour barbeque sauce evenly over the dough.
6. Add **cooked** chicken meat.
7. Sprinkle with cheese.
8. Bake for 20 minutes.

Makes 1 Pizza

Deep Dish Pizza

Ingredients:
- 2 tablespoons all-purpose flour
- 1/8 teaspoon baking powder
- 1 dash salt
- 1 teaspoon softened butter
- 2 1/4 teaspoons milk
- 1 tablespoon pizza sauce
- 1 1/4 tablespoons shredded mozzarella cheese

Directions:
1. Stir together flour, baking powder, salt and butter until dough looks like medium-sized crumbs.
2. Slowly add milk while stirring.
3. Shape the dough into a ball and place onto a buttered pan.
4. Use your fingers to pat the dough evenly over the bottom of the pan, then up the sides.
5. Pour the sauce evenly over the dough.
6. Sprinkle with the cheese.
7. Bake about 20 minutes.
8. Remove from oven.

Makes 1 pizza

English Muffin Pizza

Note:

If you plan to use ground meat or sausage in this recipe, ensure it is **cooked** first. Don't assume your oven will cook meat but it will warm cooked meat nicely.

Ingredients:
- 1 sliced English muffin
- Ready-made spaghetti sauce
- Shredded mozzarella cheese

Pre-Cooked Toppings:
- Pepperoni
- **Cooked** ground meat (optional)
- **Cooked** sausage
- Sliced mushrooms
- Peppers
- Onions

Directions:
1. Place 1/2 of the English muffin in each of 2 cake pans.
2. Top each with about 1 tablespoon of spaghetti sauce.
3. Top with any additional pre-cooked toppings.
4. Top with shredded cheese.
5. Bake for about 15-20 minutes.

Makes 2 pizzas

Ham & Cheese Bagel

Note:

Do not toast bagels in your oven. Most bagels will not fit inside & may get stuck.

Store bought deli ham is already cooked. Your oven will warm it nicely.

Ingredients:
- 1 toasted bagel cut in half.
- 1 slice of deli ham.
- 2 tablespoons cheese of your choice

Directions:
1. Place ham slice on top of toasted bagel half.
2. Warm the cheese in a warming cup.
3. Cover, stirring occasionally until warm.
4. Drizzle warm cheese on top of ham.
5. Cover with other toasted bagel half.

Ham and Spinach Quiche

Store bought deli ham is already cooked. Your oven will warm it nicely.

Ingredients:
- 1 1/3 cups sifted all-purpose flour
- 1/4 teaspoon salt
- 1/4 cup + 4 tablespoons cold, cubed, unsalted butter
- 4 - 5 tablespoons ice cold water

Filling Ingredients:
- 2 eggs
- 1/4 cup cream
- 1/8 cup deli ham, diced
- 1/4 cup grated cheese
- 1/4 cup chopped spinach
- Salt and freshly ground black pepper to taste

Directions:
1. In a medium bowl, stir together the flour and the salt.
2. Using a pastry cutter, cut in the butter until the mixture resembles coarse crumbles.
3. Sprinkle the water, 1 tablespoon at a time, over the flour mixture and toss together with a fork until the dough starts to form. The dough should be slightly sticky or tacky.
4. Form the dough into a round shape.
5. Wrap in waxed paper and chill in the refrigerator for at least 30 minutes before using.

Filling directions:
1. Put all ingredients in a medium mixing bowl.
2. Stir together until thoroughly combined.
3. On a lightly floured surface, roll out the crust to 1/8 inch thickness.
4. Use a small pan to cut out one layer of dough per quiche.
5. Butter a round pan then press the dough into the bottom and up the sides.

6. Place two to three tablespoons of the filling in the center of the quiche dough.
7. Bake for about 30 minutes.
8. Repeat with the other quiches.

Lasagna

Ingredients:
- 4 ounces cooked lasagna noodles
- 1 cube ricotta cheese
- 1/2 cup mozzarella cheese
- 1 beaten egg
- Spaghetti sauce

Directions:
1. Pour sauce over the bottom of a pan and put aside.
2. Mix cheeses and egg in bowl.
3. Lay a cooked lasagna noodle on a flat surface.
4. Spread some of cheese/egg mixture on one side of the noodle, leaving room at the ends and sides of the noodle so cheese won't ooze out when you roll it up.
5. Roll the noodle and place it edge down in the oven pan.
6. Pour spaghetti sauce on top.
7. Bake for about 15 minutes.
8. Repeat with remaining noodles.

Quesadillas

Your oven will not cook meat. Use only **cooked** chicken in this recipe.

Ingredients:
- 1 teaspoon butter
- 2 flour or corn tortillas
- Grated cheddar cheese or Jack cheese

Optional (to add a little spice to your quesadillas):
- Olives
- Salsa
- Chopped **cooked** chicken pieces
- Other chopped vegetables

Directions:
1. Melt the butter in a warming cup.
2. Carefully brush one side of a tortilla with half the melted butter.
3. Turn tortilla over.
4. Top with grated cheese.
5. Place the other tortilla on top, creating a sandwich of cheese.
6. Brush the remaining melted butter on top of the tortilla.
7. Cut into quarters and place in a baking pan.
8. Bake one quarter at a time until cheese is melted and top is brown.
9. Repeat with other quarters and serve.
10. Add any optional items.
11. Top with grated cheese.

PIES

Apple Pie

Ingredients:
- 1/3 cup pie crust mix (such as Betty Crocker or Jiffy)
- 4 teaspoons water
- 6 teaspoons apple pie filling

Directions:
1. In a bowl, combine pie crust mix and water with a fork, stirring gently to form a ball.
2. Divide the dough in half and form 2 smaller balls.
3. On a floured surface, roll out one ball slightly larger than the pan.
4. Fit into buttered pan.
5. Fill with pie filling.
6. Roll out the second ball of dough and place on top of the filling.
7. Seal edges with a fork.
8. Bake for 25 to 30 minutes.

Blueberry Pie

Ingredients:
- 1/3 cup pie crust mix (such as Betty Crocker or Jiffy)
- 4 teaspoons water
- 6 teaspoons blueberry pie filling

Directions:
1. In a bowl, combine pie crust mix and water with a fork, stirring gently to form a ball.
2. Divide the dough in half, forming 2 small balls.
3. On a floured surface, roll out one ball slightly larger than the pan.
4. Fit into greased pan.
5. Fill with pie filling.
6. Roll out second ball of dough, place on top of the filling.
7. Seal edges with a fork.
8. Bake for 25 to 30 minutes.

Cherry Pie

Ingredients:
- 1/3 cup pie crust mix (such as Betty Crocker or Jiffy)
- 4 teaspoons water
- 6 teaspoons cherry pie filling

Directions:
1. In a small bowl, combine pie crust mix and water with fork, stirring gently to form a ball.
2. Divide the dough in half, forming 2 small balls.
3. On a floured board roll out one ball slightly larger than the pan.
4. Fit into greased pan.
5. Fill with pie filling.
6. Roll out second ball of dough, place on top of the filling.
7. Seal edges with a fork.
8. Bake for 25 to 30 minutes.

Lemon Whipped Cream Pie

Ingredients:
- 1 prepared sugar cookie mix
- 1 teaspoon egg yolk
- 2 teaspoons lemon juice
- 3 tablespoons sweetened condensed milk
- 1/8 teaspoon grated lemon rind
- Whipped cream

Directions:
1. Butter an oven cake pan.
2. Make sugar cookie recipe.
3. Press into pan and up sides.
4. Bake for 5 minutes and remove from the oven.
5. While it's baking, mix together the egg yolk, lemon juice and condensed milk.
6. Sprinkle the grated lemon rind over the egg mixture.
7. Pour the mixture into the hot sugar cookie.
8. Bake for 12 minutes.
9. Allow to cool completely in pan.
10. Add whipped cream on top.
11. Serve

Oreo Butterscotch Pie

Ingredients:
- 1/3 cup Oreo cookie crumbs
- 1 teaspoon cocoa
- 1 tablespoon sweetened condensed milk
- 1/8 teaspoon milk
- 2 tablespoons butterscotch chips
- Chopped nuts

Directions:
1. Butter an oven pan.
2. Combine all ingredients and blend thoroughly.
3. Spread mixture into pan
4. Bake about 10 minutes.

Strawberry Pie

Ingredients:
- 1/3 cup pie crust mix (such as Betty Crocker or Jiffy)
- 4 teaspoons water
- 2 tablespoons strawberry pie filling

Directions:
1. In a small bowl, combine pie crust mix and water with fork, stirring gently to form a ball.
2. Divide the dough in half, forming 2 small balls.
3. On a floured board roll out one ball slightly larger than the pan.
4. Fit into greased pan.
5. Fill with pie filling.
6. Roll out second ball of dough, place on top.
7. Seal edges with a fork.
8. Bake for 25 to 30 minutes.

SNACKS and DESSERTS

Baked Apple with Cheese

Ingredients:
- 1 large apple
- 2 tablespoons shredded cheddar cheese

Directions:
1. Wash the apple and remove its center core.
2. Slice across the apple to make rings about 1/2 inch thick.
3. Butter a pan.
4. Place apple slice(s) in pan one at a time.
5. Add cheese.
6. Bake each slice about 15 minutes.

Baked Cinnamon Apple

Ingredients:
- 1 large apple
- 1/4 teaspoon butter
- 1/8 teaspoon cinnamon
- 1 tablespoon sugar

Directions:
1. Wash a large apple and remove its center core.
2. Slice across the apple to make 1/2" thick rings.
3. Butter a pan.
4. Place apple slice(s) in pan one at a time.
5. Sprinkle lightly with cinnamon.
6. Sprinkle lightly with sugar.
7. Top with butter.
8. Bake about 20 minutes.

Banana Split Pizza

Ingredients:
- 1 prepared sugar cookie dough
- Whipped cream
- 2 tablespoons sliced banana
- 2 tablespoons fresh sliced strawberries
- 2 tablespoons drained crushed pineapple
- 2 tablespoons halved seedless grapes

Directions:
1. Press cookie dough evenly an oven pan.
2. Bake for 15 to 20 minutes, until golden brown.
3. Cool in pan on wire rack.
4. Spread whipped topping over cooled crust.
5. Arrange fruit in a decorative pattern.
6. Refrigerate until ready to serve.

Cinnamon Crisps

Ingredients:
- 1/2 cup flour
- 1/4 teaspoon salt
- 3 teaspoons butter
- 1 tablespoon ice water
- Cinnamon
- Sugar
- Jam; optional

Directions:
1. Combine flour, salt and butter with a fork.
2. Sprinkle with ice water and stir gently until dough forms a ball.
3. Roll dough out on lightly floured surface until about 1/8-inch thick.
4. Sprinkle with cinnamon and sugar.
5. Cut into desired shapes.
6. Place on an ungreased pan.
7. Bake until lightly browned.
8. Spread jam on top.

Dessert Pizza

Ingredients:
Cookie Dough:
- 7 teaspoons butter
- 7 teaspoons sugar
- A pinch of salt
- 1/4 cup flour
- 1/8 teaspoon baking powder
- 1/8 teaspoon vanilla

Cream Cheese Spread:
- 1/4 cup sugar
- 1/4 teaspoon vanilla
- 1/4 cup cream cheese at room temperature

Other Toppings:
- Slices of banana, strawberry, blueberry or your choice of others fruits
- Mini chocolate chips

Directions: (Preheat your oven for 20 minutes)
Cookie Dough:
1. Cream the butter, sugar and salt together.
2. Add flour, baking powder and vanilla and mix into a ball of dough.
3. Roll out cookie dough on a floured surface.
4. Cut into 1-inch circles.
5. Place onto buttered pan.
6. Bake for 5 minutes.
7. Wait until cool then remove from oven.

Cream Cheese and Fruit Topping:
1. Mix together sugar, vanilla and cream cheese until smooth.
2. Spread over cookie dough.
3. Add sliced fruit of choice.
4. Add mini chocolate chips.
5. Return to oven for 8 – 10 minutes.

Fruit S'Mores

Ingredients:
- 1 tablespoon mini chocolate chips
- 2 teaspoons marshmallows cream
- 2 graham crackers
- Slices of banana, blueberry or strawberry or your choice of others fruits

Directions:
1. Preheat oven for 20 minutes.
2. Fill one warming cup halfway with mini chocolate chips.
3. Put marshmallow cream in the other warming cup.
4. Warm both cups in your oven for 6 - 9 minutes, stirring each occasionally.
5. Remove cups from oven.
6. Place fruit slices onto 1 graham cracker.
7. Pour chocolate over it, then the marshmallow.
8. Top with the remaining graham cracker.

Krispie Treats

Ingredients:
- 1 teaspoon butter
- 1 large marshmallow
- 2 tablespoons Rice Krispies cereal

Directions:
1. Place butter and marshmallow in a warming cup.
2. Cover and put on warming tray.
3. Warm the mixture for nine minutes, stirring occasionally.
4. Thoroughly mix cereal with warmed marshmallow mixture in bowl.
5. Using small amounts, form cookie shapes.
6. Place shapes on plate.
7. Refrigerate for 1/2 hour or until firm.

Peanut Butter Fudge Mix

Ingredients:
- 1 cup powdered sugar
- 5 teaspoons milk
- 1 teaspoon butter
- 1/2 teaspoon vanilla
- 4 teaspoons cocoa
- 6 teaspoons peanut butter

Directions:
1. Mix sugar, milk, butter, vanilla, and cocoa until smooth into a batter.
2. Butter two baking pans.
3. Spoon some batter into pans about 1/4-inch deep.
4. Spread 3 teaspoons peanut butter over mix.
5. Spoon another 1/4-inch thick layer of batter over the peanut butter.
6. Bake each pan about 5 minutes.
7. Let cool for 15 minutes.
8. Cut into fudge pieces.

Made in the USA
Coppell, TX
28 October 2019